I0759942

CROSSING THE FINISH LINE

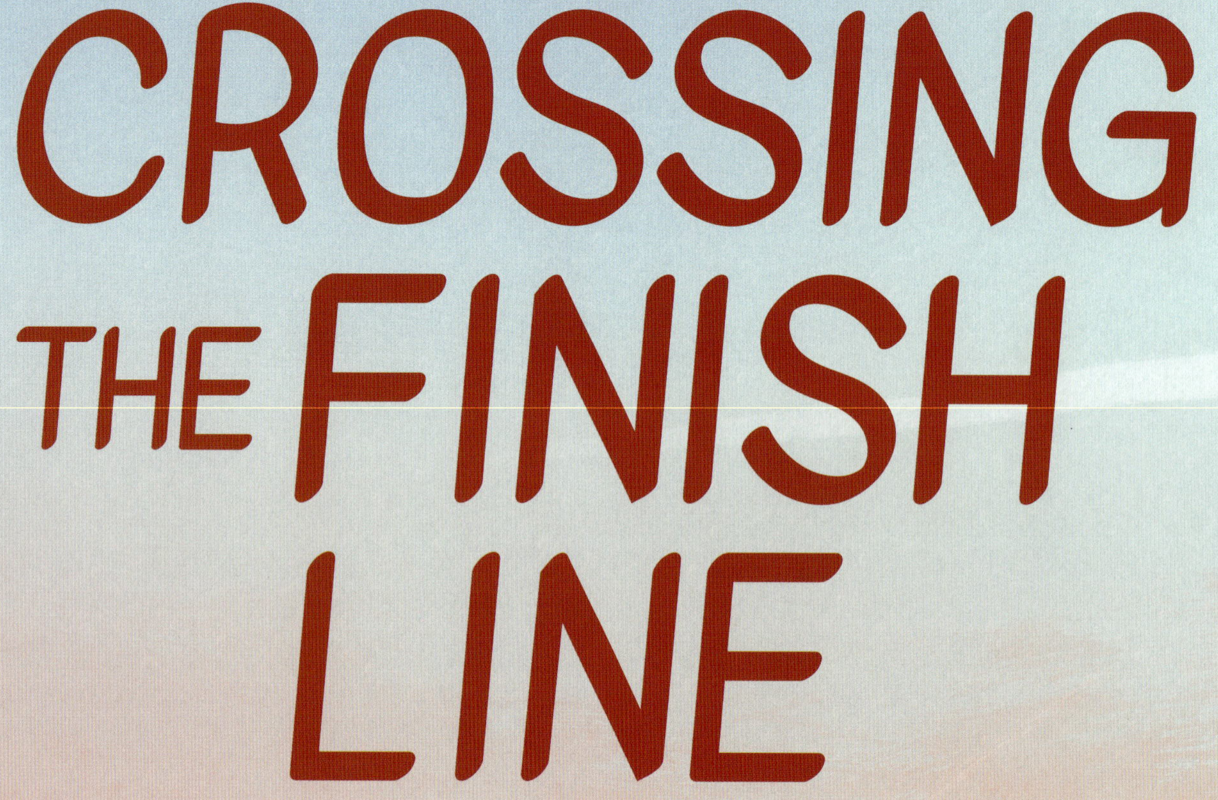

STORY BY THUSHANTHI PONWEERA

ART BY MAITHILI JOSHI

union square kids
NEW YORK

67

Ranatunge Karunananda is brown.

Sri Lankan brown.

A country and color that aren't well-known.

All this changes at the Summer Olympics of 1964.

TOKYO
64
67

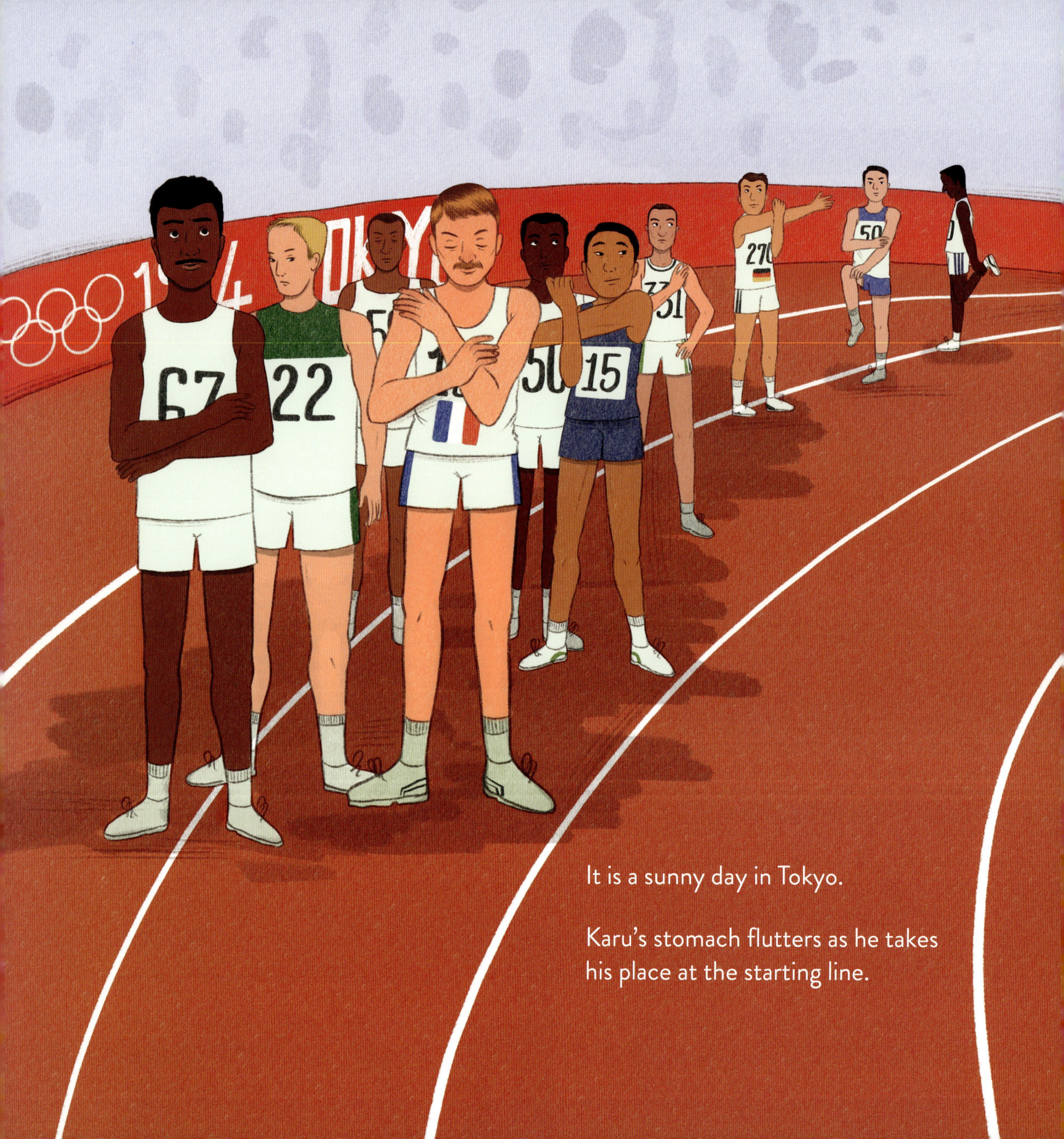

It is a sunny day in Tokyo.

Karu's stomach flutters as he takes his place at the starting line.

He is about to run 10,000 meters in the biggest stadium he has ever seen.

It is a dream come true.

Karu has always wanted
to be an athlete.

As a child, he raced with his friends,
soil and stones poking his bare feet,
ignoring the cries asking him to slow down.

He grew up to be Sri Lanka's fastest runner, breaking multiple national records.

Now he stands among the *world's* fastest runners.

A voice bellows through the speakers.

ON YOUR MARKS!

Karu shifts into position.

GET SET!

He takes a deep breath.

BOOM!

They are off!

The runners swarm around him, moving as one.
Their breath matches the rhythm of their feet slapping the ground.

As they approach the end of the first round they speed up,
some reaching it sooner than others.

Lap two,

Lap three,

Lap four.

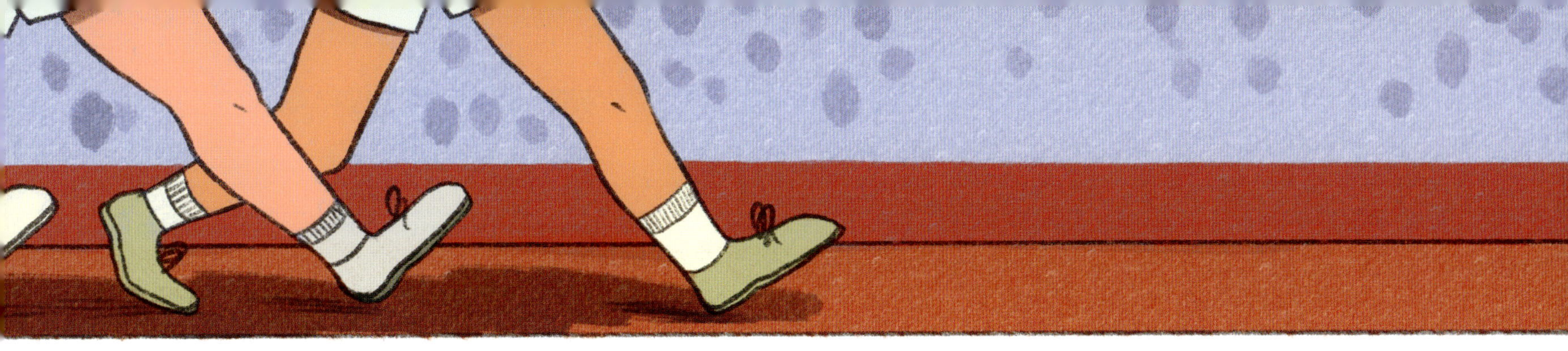

One down, twenty-four more to go.

Karu counts under his breath.

He cheers himself on as he completes each lap,
his mind focused on the track ahead.

Running is a meditation, a way to control his thoughts.

Seven.

Eight.

Nine.

The sun is blazing, and sweat drips down Karu's back.

He is familiar with the heat and humidity—it reminds him of home!

67

TUNISIA
USA! USA!
6

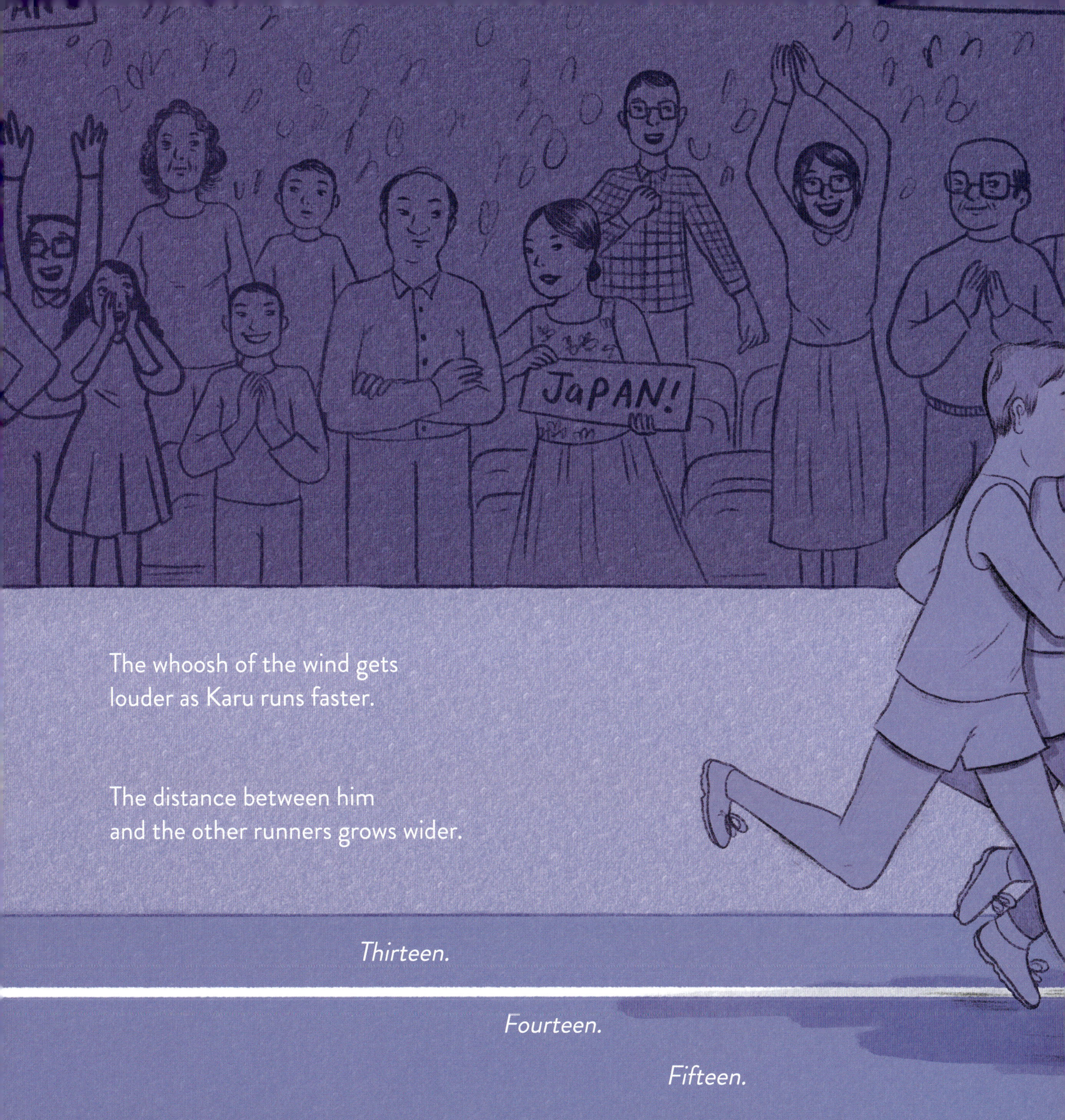

The whoosh of the wind gets louder as Karu runs faster.

The distance between him and the other runners grows wider.

Thirteen.

Fourteen.

Fifteen.

Karu can't hear the panting of his competitors anymore.

He sees their figures getting smaller in the distance.

Can he ever catch up?

Seventeen.

Eighteen.

23
37

Nineteen.

Now Karu is ahead of the swarm once more!
But it isn't because he is winning . . .
it's because he is losing!

Karu's spirits sink; his resolve weakens.
He closes his eyes and . . .

. . . there they are—his family.

He feels their warmth
as they hug him goodbye,
hears their whispered wishes.

"Go and come safely."
"We'll be waiting for you."

Whether or not he wins today,
Karu knows they are proud
of him just the same.

There is someone else
waiting for Karu too.

Someone who will
follow his example.

The sinking feeling
in his heart lifts.

Karu opens his eyes
with renewed resolve.

The comfort of the memory
pushes him forward.

Lap twenty.

Just five more,
Karu tells himself.

A runner bursts ahead of him and a voice bellows through the speakers.

"First place!"

"Second place!"

"Third place!"

Karu can't help smiling as he runs past the winners, basking for a moment in their joy.

Twenty-one.

The announcements keep coming—the names and countries of every runner to complete the race and the names of those who give up running a race they will never win.

Twenty-two.

Karu keeps on running.

Even though he is running alone,
even though he doesn't have to.

Karu's muscles ache, begging him to stop.
He needs to rest.

The winners clench their teeth, willing him to stop. They are impatient to wear their medals.

The crowd boos and jeers,
demanding he stop.
They want the race to end.

Karu notices a familiar flag—a sight that
makes the breath catch in his throat.

It is the flag of his country.

A country he serves with pride,
a country that is big in spirit—
the spirit of resilience.

Twenty-three.

By now, Karu's heart is thumping and pumping loudly.

So loudly that he doesn't notice the hush that sweeps through the crowd.

Twenty-four.

Suddenly, a loud clap rings through the silence.

Then another,

and another.

Soon the entire audience is on their feet clapping, and cheering—no, roaring! All for Karu!

The energy in the air shifts and Karu forgets his pain. He keeps running, getting closer and closer until . . .

Twenty-five.

. . . he crosses the finish line!

The cheers are deafening!

Karu soaks in the admiration as happiness
streams into every part of him.
He is last . . .

. . . but it is everything he imagined being first would feel like.

67

ABOUT RANATUNGE KARUNANANDA

Ranatunge Jayasekara Koralage Karunananda, "Karu" for short, was born on May 21, 1936 in a village called Gampola in Sri Lanka (then called Ceylon). Although he joined the Sri Lankan Army, he held on to his childhood dream of becoming an elite athlete and trained to make it a reality. His hard work paid off—he was the only runner on a team of six competitors that represented Sri Lanka at the 1964 Summer Olympics.

On the day of the 10,000 meter race Karu, wearing bib number 67, was suffering from a bad cold. But he was driven by his sense of responsibility to his country and to his family. That and his belief that "Participating is more important than winning," was what motivated him to complete the race. Karu's relatable spirit of persistence and discipline won the hearts of the Japanese people, who hailed him on TV and in newspapers as "the most spirited loser."

AUTHOR'S NOTE

I hadn't heard of Karu's story until a few years ago, when a video of him went viral online. Upon learning that he never received the same attention and appreciation that Japan showed him from his own country before his death in 1974, I was determined to share his legacy with people around the world. It is said that Pierre de Coubertin, the founder of the modern Olympics, believed that the most important part of the Games was not just winning, but taking part. He recognized that what matters in life is not conquering challenges, but doing your best, and I can think of no other person to have done justice to this sentiment better than Karu.

So, when you feel like giving up—when your dreams feel so close but also so far away—I hope you remember Karu and see things through to the end. Because who knows? It might be disappointing, but it also might be . . . *amazing*.

For my parents, Ajanthi & Vijitha,
for always cheering me on.
—T. P.

For my family.
—M. J.

union square kids
NEW YORK

UNION SQUARE KIDS and the distinctive Union Square Kids logo are trademarks of Union Square & Co., LLC.

Union Square & Co., LLC, is a subsidiary of Sterling Publishing Co., Inc.

Text © 2025 Thushanthi Ponweera
Cover and interior art © 2025 Maithili Joshi

All rights reserved. No part of this publication may be reproduced, stored in a retrieval system, or transmitted in any form or by any means (including electronic, mechanical, photocopying, recording, or otherwise) without prior written permission from the publisher.

Any trademarks, names, logos, and designs are the property of their owners. Unless specifically identified as such, use herein of any third-party trademarks, company names, or celebrity or personal names, likenesses, images, or quotations, does not indicate any relationship, sponsorship, or endorsement between the author, the publisher, and the trademark owner, company, celebrity, or person.

ISBN 978-1-4549-5018-9

Library of Congress Cataloging-in-Publication Data

Names: Ponweera, Thushanthi, author. | Joshi, Maithili, illustrator.
Title: Crossing the finish line / words by Thushanthi Ponweera ; illustrated by Maithili Joshi.
Description: New York, N.Y. : Union Square Kids, 2025. | Audience: Ages 4-8 | Summary: "A nonfiction picture book about the courage and perseverance of 1964 Sri Lankan Olympian, Ranatunge Karunananda, and the ways in which we define success"-- Provided by publisher.
Identifiers: LCCN 2023053881 | ISBN 9781454950189 (hardcover)
Subjects: LCSH: Karunananda, 1936-1975--Juvenile literature. | Courage--Juvenile literature. | Perseverance (Ethics)--Juvenile literature. | Olympic athletes--Sri Lanka--Biography--Juvenile literature. | Long-distance runners--Sri Lanka--Biography--Juvenile literature.
Classification: LCC GV1061.15.K393 P66 2025 | DDC 796.42/4092 [B]--dc23/eng/20240416
LC record available at https://lccn.loc.gov/2023053881

For information about custom editions, special sales, and premium purchases, please contact specialsales@unionsquareandco.com.

Printed in China

Lot #:
2 4 6 8 10 9 7 5 3 1

02/25

unionsquareandco.com

Cover and interior design by Julie Robine